W9-CNA-364

WHAT DOES A
POWER FORWARD
DO?

Paul Challen

PowerKiDS press™

New York

Published in 2017 by The Rosen Publishing Group, Inc.
29 East 21st Street, New York, NY 10010

Developed and Produced for Rosen by BlueApple*Works* Inc.
Managing Editor for BlueApple*Works*: Melissa McClellan
Art Director: Tibor Choleva
Designer: Joshua Avramson
Photo Research: Jane Reid
Editor: Kelly Spence

Basketball is a fluid game; care was taken and every effort was made to portray players in
the identified positions to highlight the content being featured.

Photo Credits: Title page, page borders michelaubryphoto/Shutterstock; title page, p. 7, 10, 11, 12, 13, 16, 18, 19, 20, 21, 22, 23, 24
Aspenphoto/Shutterstock.com; page backgrounds Eugene Sergeev/Shutterstock; TOC Aleksandar Grozdanovski/Shutterstock;
p. 4 T.J. Choleva /EKS/Shutterstock; p. 5 Eric Broder Van Dyke/Dreamstime.com; p. 6, 14 Debby Wong/Shutterstock.com; p. 8
Jupiterimages/Thinkstock; p. 9 Richard Kane/Dreamstime.com; p. 15 Louis Horch/Dreamstime.com; p. 17 Blulz60/Shutterstock.com;
p. 17 top Lipofsky Basketballphoto.com/Creative Commons; p. 21 top Keith Allison/Creative Commons; p. 25 Steve Debenport/
iStockphoto; p. 26 left Verse Photography/Creative Commons; p. 26 right Natursports/Dreamstime.com; p. 27 left Photo Works/
Shutterstock.com; p. 27 right Edward A. Ornelas/ ZUMAPRESS.com; p. 28 Monkey Business Images/Shutterstock; p. 29 Cosmin
Iftode/Dreamstime.com

Cataloging-in-Publication Data
Names: Challen, Paul.
Title: What does a power forward do? / Paul Challen.
Description: New York : PowerKids Press, 2017. | Series: Basketball smarts | Includes index.
Identifiers: ISBN 9781508150510 (pbk.) | ISBN 9781508150466 (library bound) |
    ISBN 9781508150343 (6 pack)
Subjects: LCSH: Forwards (Basketball)--Juvenile literature. | Basketball--Offense--
    Juvenile literature.
Classification: LCC GV889.C53 2017 | DDC 796.323--dc23

Manufactured in the United States of America
CPSIA Compliance Information: Batch #BS16PK For Further Information contact: Rosen Publishing, New York, New York at 1-800-237-9932

CONTENTS

THE BASKETBALL TEAM

During a basketball game, teams battle for the win with five players on each side. Each player on a team has an assigned position on the court. The five positions include point guard, shooting guard, small forward, power forward, and center. The players in these positions have different jobs to do, both on **offense**, when their team has the ball, and on **defense**, when their opponents do.

Each position is assigned a number. This diagram shows where each player is typically positioned when the team is trying to score.

1. Point guard: *The player who is responsible for leading the team and creating scoring opportunities.*

2. Shooting guard: *A player who focuses on scoring baskets, often from a **wing**, or side, position.*

3. Small forward: *A speedy, skilled player who can score baskets.*

4. Power forward: *A player who uses their size to play close to the basket to **rebound** and defend.*

5. Center: *Usually the tallest player on the team, the center plays near the net and shoots, rebounds, and blocks shots.*

To score baskets on offense, players move the ball as a team by **dribbling** and **passing**. They use plays to set up openings to take shots on the basket. On defense, teammates work together to stop their opponents from scoring. It is important for a team to combine both the offensive and defensive parts of the sport. All good basketball teams use **strategy** and teamwork to play a well-balanced game.

*The power forward (marked with a yellow arrow throughout this book) is considered a **post** player. Post players tend to stick close to the basket on both offense and defense.*

THE FOUR-SPOT

On the basketball court, the power forward is often called the "four." The power forward joins the small forward and the center in the **frontcourt** of a basketball team. As the name suggests, the player in this position must be big and strong, and is often the second-tallest player on the team. The power forward must enjoy playing a physical game, whether shooting, rebounding, or playing defense.

The power forward is often tasked with tough jobs, such as setting **screens**, diving for loose balls, and **boxing out** opponents to gain position for rebounds.

DID YOU KNOW?

Some power forwards combine the strength and physical play of this position with the all-around skills of a small forward. This player, who fans sometimes call a "stretch four," has the skills to play farther from the basket. A stretch four can make long-range shots and has the ability to dribble and drive to the basket. These moves help pull defenders out of the key, allowing a team to spread out on the court.

The power forward almost always plays close to the basket. On offense, this player usually looks for shots close to the basket, using their size to take high-percentage shots from inside the **key**. On defense, the power forward is usually responsible for guarding the player in the same position on the opposing team—meaning a lot of pushing and physical play.

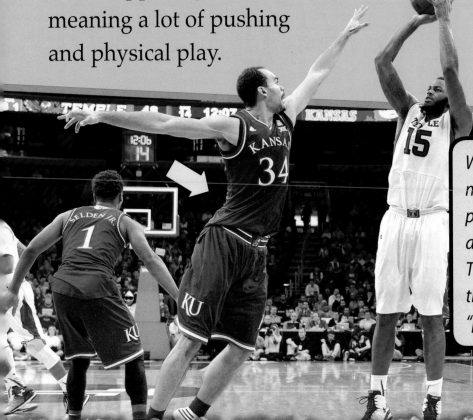

While the power forward might not be the tallest player on the team, they are often very muscular. This strength is part of the reason they're called "power" forwards!

OFFENSIVE STRATEGY

A half-court offense relies on a strong power forward. In this offensive attack, players pass the ball among their teammates in the opponents' half of the court. The goal of this offense is to create opportunities to set up the team's "big men," the power forward and center, for high-percentage shots close to the basket.

While traditional power forwards mostly sink shots from fairly close to the basket, they usually have a bit more range than centers and are able to make shots from farther out.

A team running a half-court offense has to be patient because it can take time to move the ball around by passing and dribbling. One of the key parts of a power forward's offensive game is the **post-up** move.
This involves getting set with their back to the basket, close to the rim, with their defender falling between the power forward and the basket. The player who posts up looks to receive the ball from a teammate, then uses fast footwork and a few dribbles
to get closer to the basket
for a quick shot.

The up-and-under is a popular move for post players. In the first part of the move, players fake out their defenders by pretending they're going to shoot. When the defender jumps up to block, the shooter ducks around them to take a clear shot on net.

DEFENSIVE STRATEGY

The power forward is a key player for any team on defense. This player needs to know how to use their strength and size to "protect the paint" in the key close to the basket. Any offensive player driving through this area knows that the power forward will be there, trying to block shots and generally making it tough to score.

Power forwards try to put themselves between the player with the ball and the net. This allows them to block shots, and places them in a good position to grab rebounds.

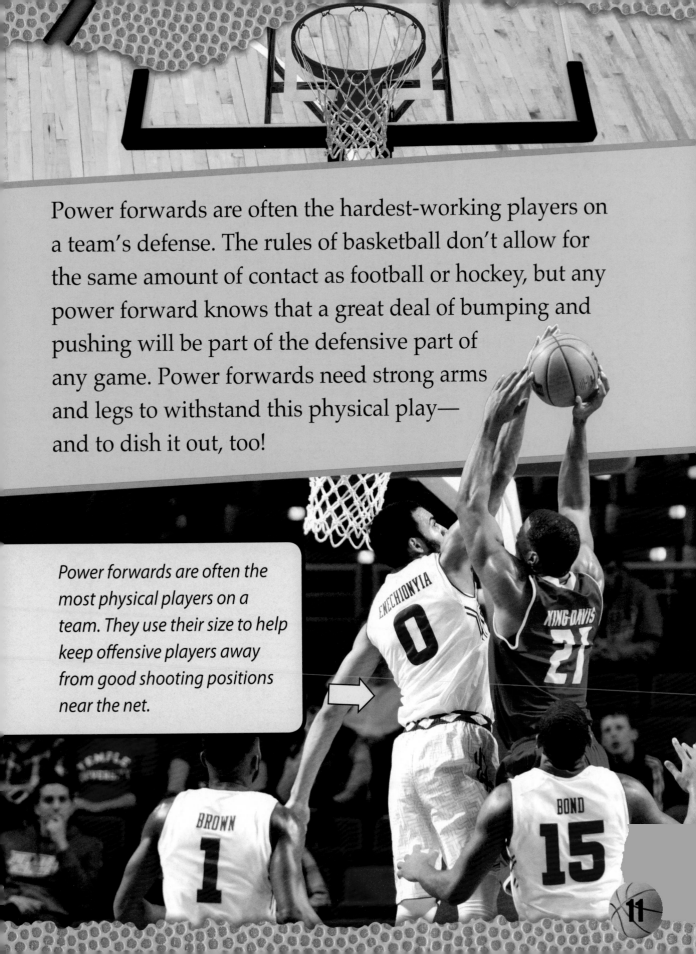

Power forwards are often the hardest-working players on a team's defense. The rules of basketball don't allow for the same amount of contact as football or hockey, but any power forward knows that a great deal of bumping and pushing will be part of the defensive part of any game. Power forwards need strong arms and legs to withstand this physical play— and to dish it out, too!

Power forwards are often the most physical players on a team. They use their size to help keep offensive players away from good shooting positions near the net.

DEFENDING THE POST

Rebounding is crucial to the success of any basketball team, and the power forward is often a team's best rebounder. Grabbing a defensive rebound is important because it means your opponent only gets one chance to shoot. Capturing an offensive rebound can give the power forward's team another shot on basket. Rebounding successfully involves good body position, the ability to legally push your opponent away from the basket, and reading how a missed shot will come off the rim or backboard.

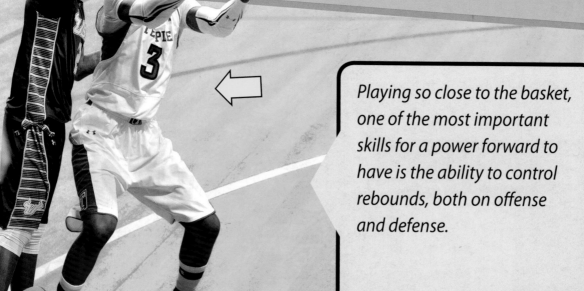

Playing so close to the basket, one of the most important skills for a power forward to have is the ability to control rebounds, both on offense and defense.

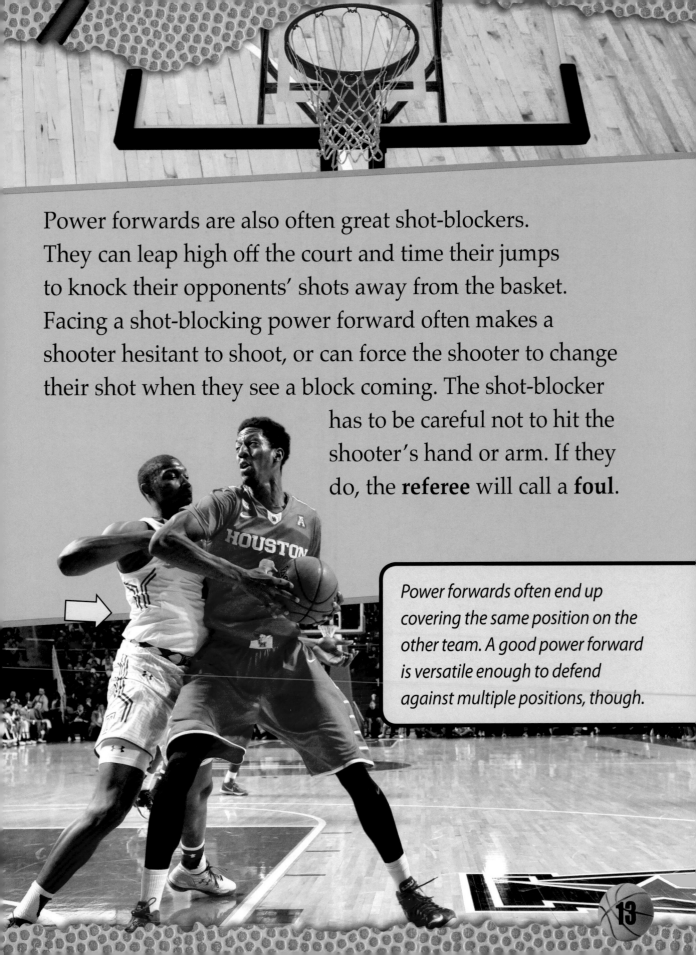

Power forwards are also often great shot-blockers. They can leap high off the court and time their jumps to knock their opponents' shots away from the basket. Facing a shot-blocking power forward often makes a shooter hesitant to shoot, or can force the shooter to change their shot when they see a block coming. The shot-blocker has to be careful not to hit the shooter's hand or arm. If they do, the **referee** will call a **foul**.

Power forwards often end up covering the same position on the other team. A good power forward is versatile enough to defend against multiple positions, though.

POWER FORWARD PLAYS

When a shot goes up, the power forward must block out opponents. Also known as boxing out, this positioning makes it tough for an opposing player to grab a rebound. As important as it is for a power forward to be strong and physical, to box out an opponent you also need to be smart and quick. To box out an opponent, the power forward must stay between their opponent and the basket, fighting for position to win the rebound.

When boxing an opponent out, power forwards plant their feet to hold their ground and use their arms to keep their opponents away from the net. They shuffle from side to side to stay in between the player and the basket.

Power forwards also need to know how to execute a successful screen. To do this, the power forward takes a position on the court in the path of a player trying to defend against a teammate who is dribbling. The defender will then run into the screening power forward, allowing the teammate to dribble past. Also known as a "pick," the player executing one can then roll to the basket (the "pick and roll") or pop out to the top of the key (the "pick and pop"), giving the ball handler options for a pass.

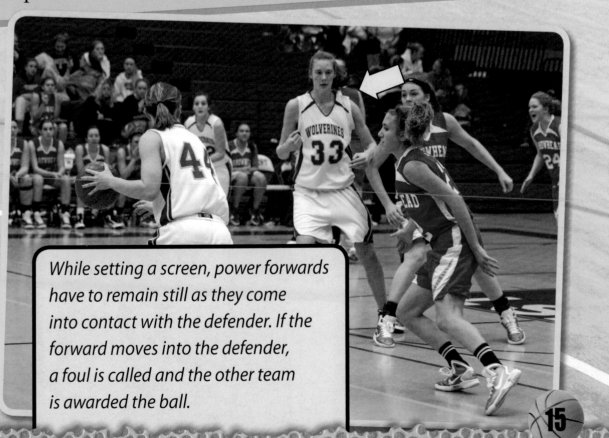

While setting a screen, power forwards have to remain still as they come into contact with the defender. If the forward moves into the defender, a foul is called and the other team is awarded the ball.

SHOOTING THE BALL

Although other players on the team may be called on to shoot more often, power forwards must be strong shooters as well. After all, it would be very easy for a team to defend against an opposing team with one player who is never a threat to score! In basketball, shooting requires a mix of strength, speed, and balance. Power forwards must be aware of what shots they can make, and when it is a better option to pass to an open teammate.

Stretch fours, with their increased range, are often called upon to shoot more than more traditional power forwards. Often these additional shots are three-pointers.

The only way for any player, including a power forward, to become a good shooter is through lots of practice. To become a professional, players must take thousands of shots in the gym, on the playground, and in the driveway, perfecting the skills needed to score from all over the court. Great shooters can make scoring look easy, but nothing could be further from the truth.

The quick shot drill is one practice technique power forwards use to improve their shooting skills. They set up in different positions near the post. After receiving a pass, they dribble once, then quickly spin around and shoot. This allows power forwards to practice the most common shot they will take in a game.

POST SHOOTING

While guards and the small forward specialize in long-range shooting, the power forward's position is effective much closer to the basket. This means that players in this position need to be skilled at making baskets close to the hoop. But just because those shots are coming from near the basket, it doesn't mean they are easy to make!

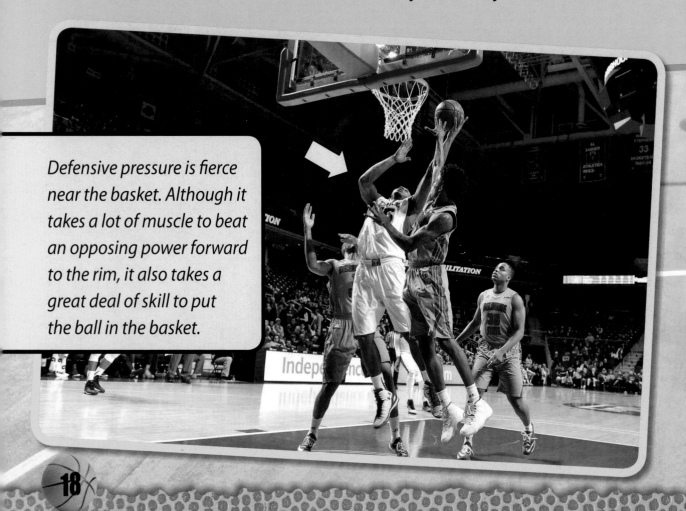

Defensive pressure is fierce near the basket. Although it takes a lot of muscle to beat an opposing power forward to the rim, it also takes a great deal of skill to put the ball in the basket.

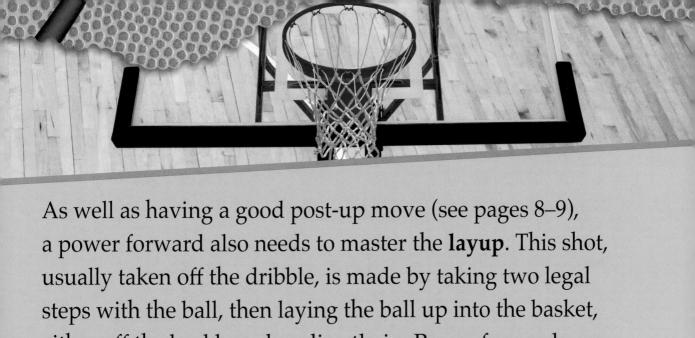

As well as having a good post-up move (see pages 8–9), a power forward also needs to master the **layup**. This shot, usually taken off the dribble, is made by taking two legal steps with the ball, then laying the ball up into the basket, either off the backboard or directly in. Power forwards are often good at **dunking**. In this exciting move, a player holds the ball, jumps up in an explosive motion, and slams the ball into the basket.

One power forward famous for his dunks was Gus "Honeycomb" Johnson (not pictured). His dunks were so powerful that he shattered three backboards throughout his career. Today, breaking a backboard is punished as a technical foul.

THE JUMP SHOT

One of the skills that can make an average power forward into a great player is the **jump shot**. Many defenders expect power forwards to try to score from close to the basket. By being able to make an outside shot, the power forward increases their opportunities to score. One of the most effective ways for a power forward to score from outside the key is with a solid jump shot.

Though the power forward is famous for playing close to the post, many are also skilled at shooting from a distance. It's not unheard of for a power forward to have an accurate shot from as far away as 18 feet (5.5 m)!

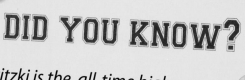

Dirk Nowitzki is the all-time high scorer for the Dallas Mavericks. Nowitzki was born in Germany and came into the NBA in 1998. He has played for the Mavericks every year since. Standing 7 feet (2.1 m) tall, Nowitzki is an excellent outside shooter, a skill that has boosted his point totals ever since his rookie season.

The jump shot is an essential part of any player's offensive game. To take a jump shot, a player leaps in the air off two feet to rise over a defender. At the top of the jump, the shooter releases the ball from high above their head, making it even harder for a defender to block the shot.

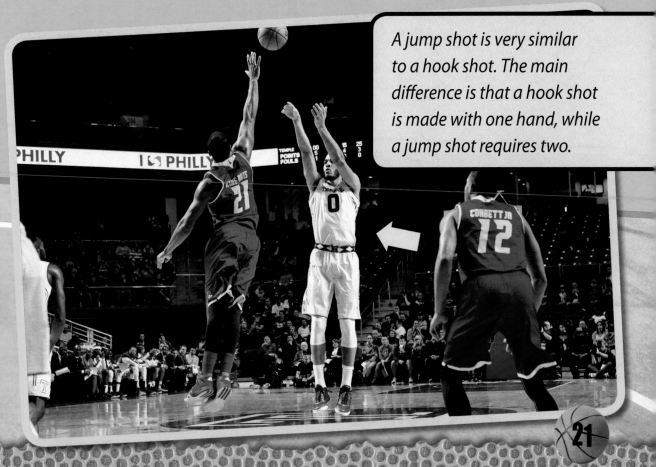

A jump shot is very similar to a hook shot. The main difference is that a hook shot is made with one hand, while a jump shot requires two.

GETTING TO THE LINE

In such a physical position, power forwards get fouled a lot, many times while taking a shot. That means that they make regular trips to the **free-throw** line in the course of a game. A power forward who can successfully sink free throws can add many points to their game totals by being good at the line. Of course, this takes a lot of practice.

Free throws are made from farther away from the net than power forwards usually shoot. It's just one of the many situations where being able to shoot from a distance comes in handy.

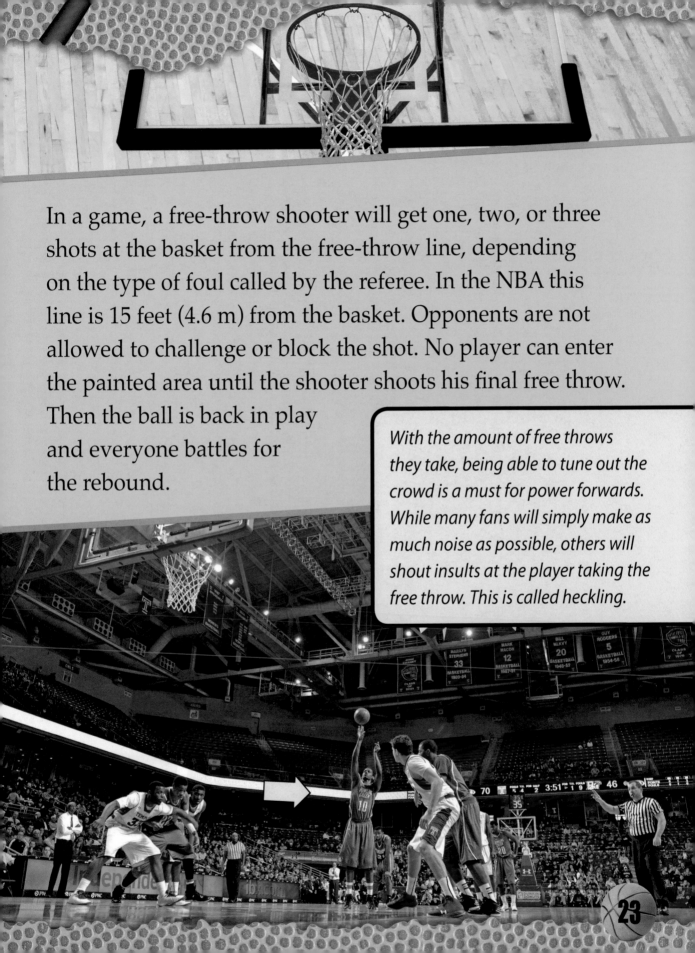

In a game, a free-throw shooter will get one, two, or three shots at the basket from the free-throw line, depending on the type of foul called by the referee. In the NBA this line is 15 feet (4.6 m) from the basket. Opponents are not allowed to challenge or block the shot. No player can enter the painted area until the shooter shoots his final free throw. Then the ball is back in play and everyone battles for the rebound.

With the amount of free throws they take, being able to tune out the crowd is a must for power forwards. While many fans will simply make as much noise as possible, others will shout insults at the player taking the free throw. This is called heckling.

THE ROLE OF A COACH

Coaches prepare their teams for games in many ways. A good coach teaches players the correct techniques for passing, shooting, dribbling, and defending. They also help players develop these skills through lots of practice. Coaches also pair the strengths of each individual player and position into a team effort. Many experts say that behind every great team there is also a great coach.

One part of a coach's job is to give a player drills that will help them improve in their position. After all, the skills a power forward needs to develop aren't necessarily the same as what a point guard has to improve on.

Coaches advise players and families about the game off the court as well. They give advice on eating a healthy diet, and the importance of rest and recovery. Because of their role as hardworking players on any team, power forwards can learn a lot about the game from a good coach.

Coaches come up with offensive and defensive plays to help their players win games. To execute a successful play, each player has to know where they need to be on the court.

THE BEST POWER FORWARDS

There have been hundreds of great power forwards. Basketball fans love to debate about who the best all-time players in this position have been. Early greats were Kevin McHale, Bob Pettit, and Elvin Hayes. Other standout power forwards include Karl Malone, Charles Barkley, Dirk Nowitzki, Kevin Garnett, and Pau Gasol.

Blake Griffin (left) of the Los Angeles Clippers is a high-flying power forward. He started playing in the NBA in 2011. That year, he won the Rookie of the Year and the NBA All-Star Game dunk competition.

The New Orleans Pelicans' Anthony Davis (right) is an impressive player. In 2012, he won an Olympic gold medal with Team USA. Davis has also played on the All-Star team three times.

Many fans consider Tim Duncan of the San Antonio Spurs to be the greatest power forward in the history of the game. Born in the US Virgin Islands, he came into the NBA in 1997 and was named that season's Rookie of the Year. Duncan has played for the Spurs every year of his pro career. Duncan combines a powerful inside game with outstanding defense. As a leader for the Spurs, he has helped the team bring home the NBA title five times during his career. He is also a two-time league MVP (2001–02, 2002–03) and has played in 15 All-Star games.

Candace Parker is a power forward with the Los Angeles Sparks in the WNBA. In 2013, she won the Best WNBA Player Espy Award. She was also only the second player to dunk in a WNBA game, ever!

BE A GOOD SPORT

Playing to win is an important part of basketball—but so is good sportsmanship. It can be easy to lose your cool on the court, so remembering to show respect for your teammates, opponents, referees, and fans is crucial. Coaches, parents, and players can make sure everyone has fun by keeping the game fair, clean, and honest.

Power forwards are part of a team, and have to know how to work together with the other players and positions to score baskets and win games.

Many power forwards have the reputation on their team as hard workers. Their dedication and work ethic can help inspire their teammates to work hard on the court, too. Power forwards can set a great example in practice and in games for their teammates so that everyone stays safe, practices good sportsmanship, and has fun.

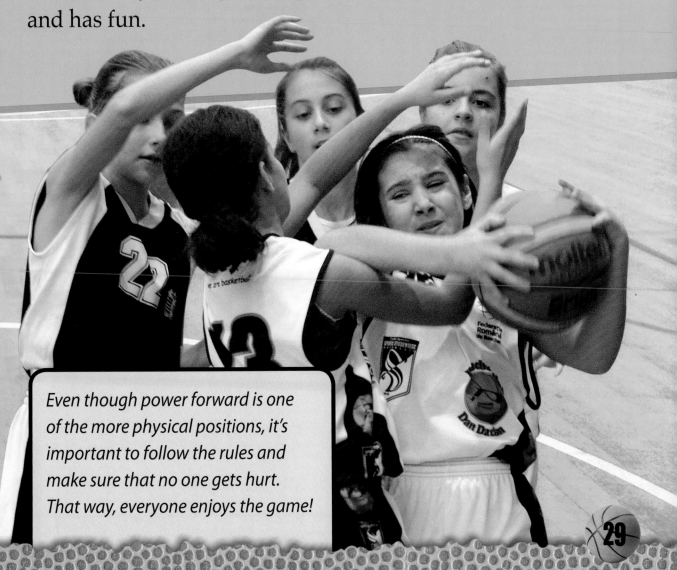

Even though power forward is one of the more physical positions, it's important to follow the rules and make sure that no one gets hurt. That way, everyone enjoys the game!

GLOSSARY

boxing out A move in which a player positions their body between an opponent and the basket to grab a rebound.

defense When a team tries to stop their opponents from scoring.

dribbling Moving the ball up the court by bouncing it with one hand.

dunking Taking a close-range shot by jumping up and slamming the ball through the hoop.

foul Committing an infraction of the rules of basketball, as determined by the referee in an official game.

free throw An uncontested shot taken from the free throw line that has been awarded after a foul.

frontcourt Where the center, small forward, and power forward play.

jump shot A shot taken by jumping off two feet and releasing the ball at the top of the jump.

key The area of a basketball court that is closest to the basket and marked off by a rectangle with a jump-ball circle at its top.

layup A moving basketball shot, taken by a player who dribbles, takes two quick steps while carrying the ball, and then shoots.

offense The part of basketball involving possession of the ball and attempts to score.

passing Throwing the ball through the air to a teammate.

post The area on a basketball court located between the basket and the free-throw line.

post up An offensive move in which a player positions himself or herself between the ball and a defender, with their back to the basket. This tactic allows for many possible shots.

rebound To catch the ball after it bounces off the rim or backboard.

referee The person who enforces the on-court rules of a basketball game.

screens Offensive moves in which one player blocks a defender so another teammate can move past.

strategy A plan to achieve a goal.

wing In basketball, one of the two sides of the court.

FOR MORE INFORMATION

FURTHER READING

Donnelly, Patrick. *The Best NBA Forwards of All Time*. Edina, MN: ABDO, 2014.

Fishman, John M. *Anthony Davis*. Minneapolis, MN: Lerner, 2016.

Gitlin, Marty. *Dirk Nowitzki: NBA Champion*. North Mankato, MN: ABDO, 2012.

Richardson, Tom. *Girls Play to Win: Basketball*. Chicago: Norwood House Press, 2011.

WEBSITES

Due to the changing nature of Internet links, PowerKids Press has developed an online list of websites related to the subject of this book. This site is updated regularly. Please use this link to access the list:

www.powerkidslinks.com/bs/pforward

INDEX